Ed Emberley's Complete FunPrint Drawing Book

 LITTLE, BROWN AND COMPANY

New York ❧ Boston ❧ London

CONTENTS

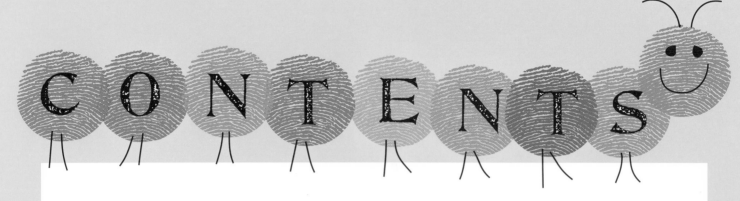

Easy! Fun!

You can make FunPrints using
your fingers or your thumbs.
Use just the tip
to make small prints.

1. Press your
finger on an
ink pad

or paint it
with watercolor
and a brush.

2. Press it on
your paper.

3. Let it dry.

4. Draw.

FOR INSTANCE

PERSON

(JUST A LINE CAN
MAKE A HAT.)

WALKING

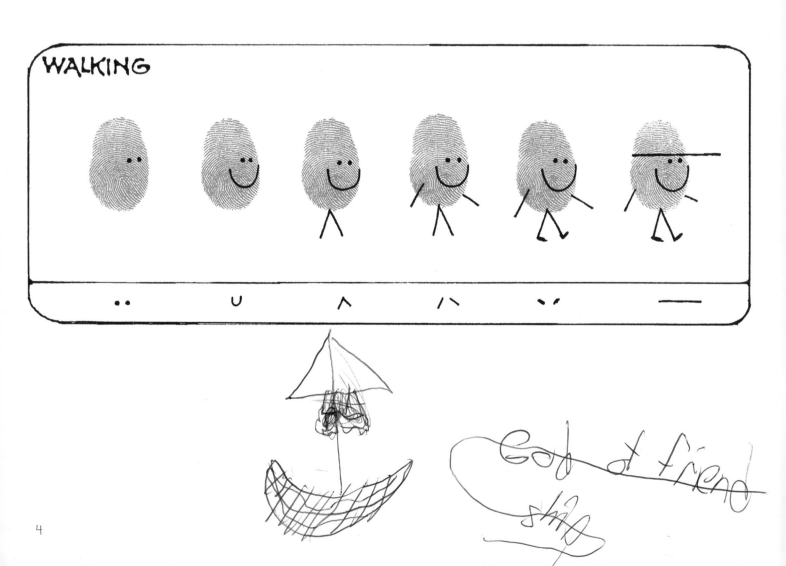

FISH

BIRD

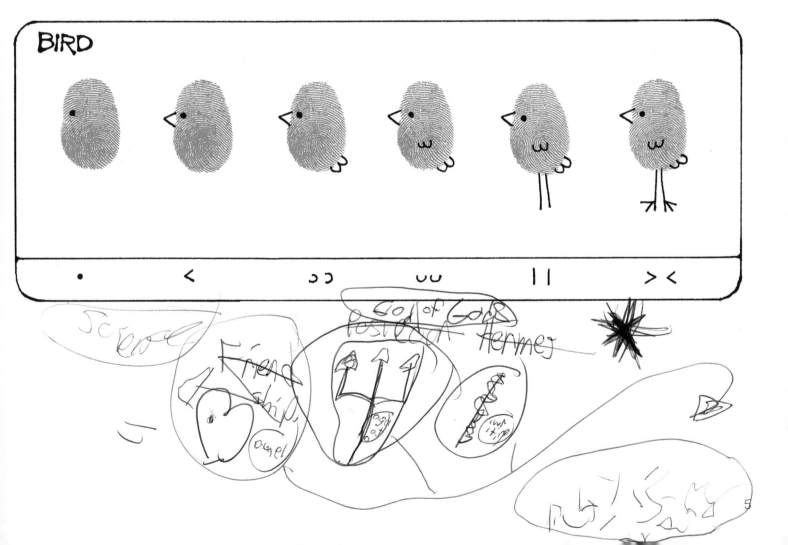

SPIDER

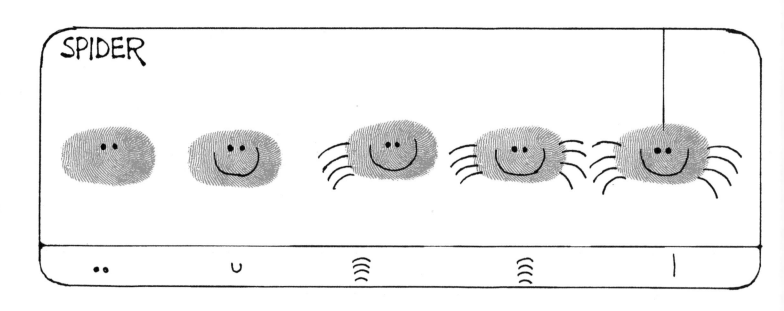

RABBIT

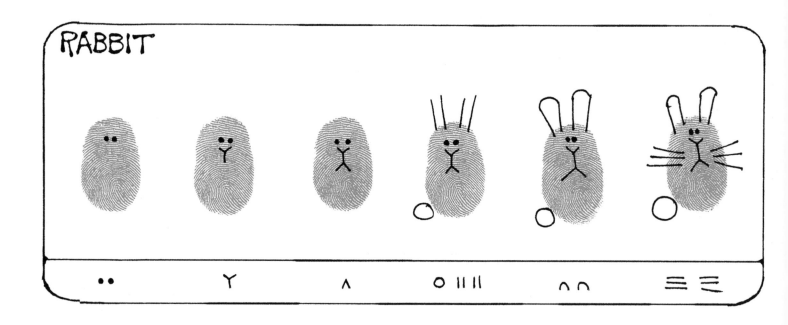

6

HALLOWEEN

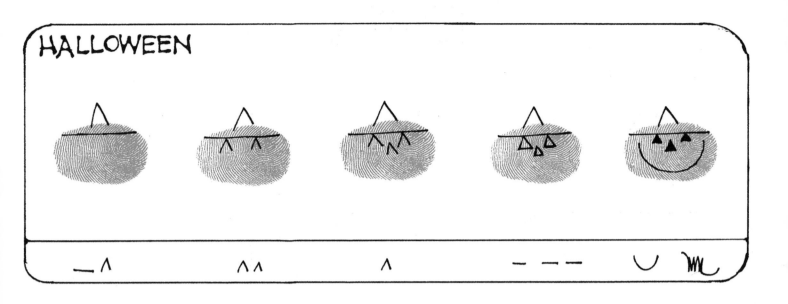

FROG

HAPPY

NOT HAPPY

LAUGHING

ANGRY

SLY

WORRIED

SHY

SPEAKING

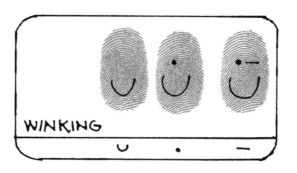

WINKING

8

SHOUTING

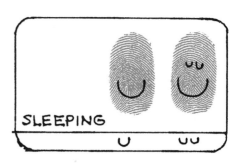

SLEEPING

WHISTLING

SCARED

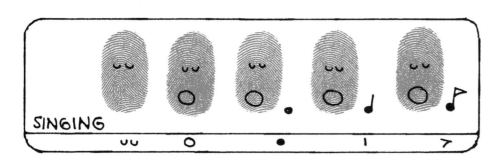

SINGING

SMILING

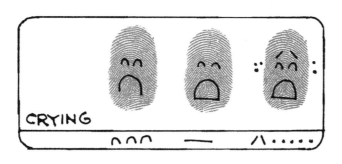

CRYING

OTHERS

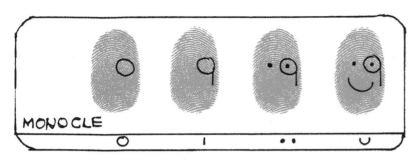

MONOCLE

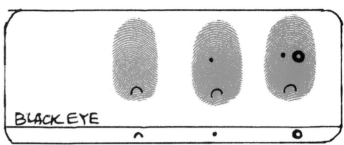

BLACK EYE

GLASSES

LOOKING AROUND

SUNGLASSES

PIRATE

DOCTOR

LOOKING AT YOU

CROOK

$$= \quad o \quad o \quad \cdot\cdot\cap \quad \text{ᴍ} \quad c \quad > \quad -\circ$$

OTHERS

HAIR

SCRIBBLES MAKE GOOD HAIR, WHISKERS, SKIRTS AND SHAGGY DOGS.

HERE ARE SOME MORE SCRIBBLES AND SOME SPECKS AND SCRATCHES.

CAP

HATS

COWBOY — ( ) COWGIRL

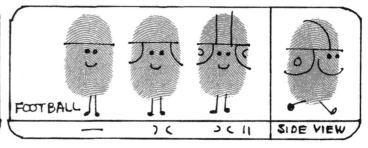

FOOTBALL —) ( ) (|| SIDE VIEW

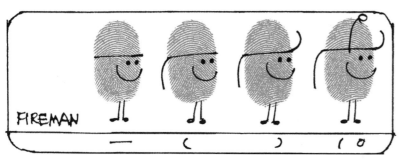

FIREMAN — ( ) (O

SKI CAPS — — O ETC.

ADMIRAL

SAILOR

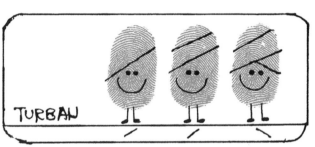

TURBAN

BAND PERSON

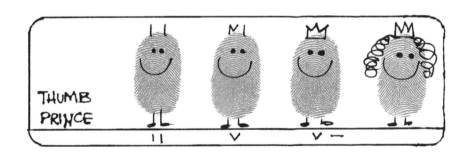

THUMB PRINCE

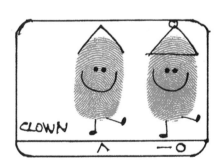

CLOWN

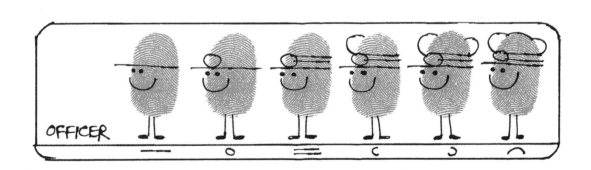

OFFICER

ACTION

WALKING

WALKING
OVER
THAT WAY →

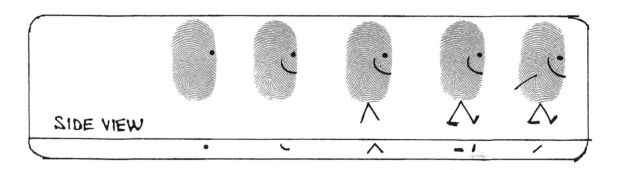

BACK VIEW

←

SIDE VIEW

RUNNING

KICKING

JUMPING

KNEELING

15

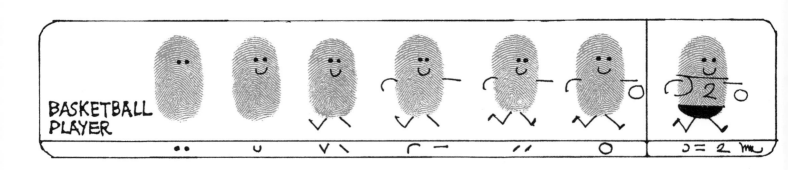

BASKETBALL PLAYER

SURFER

BOXING

ETC.

ANIMAL ACTION

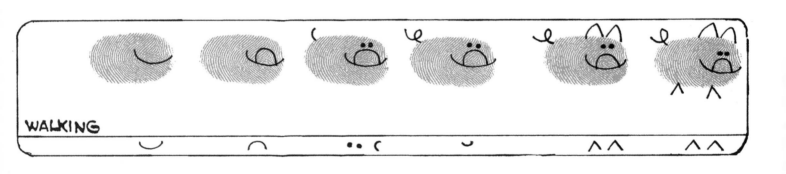

STANDING

WALKING

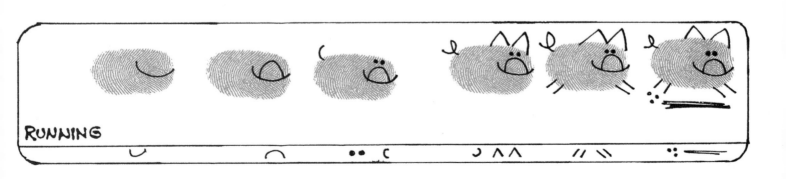

RUNNING

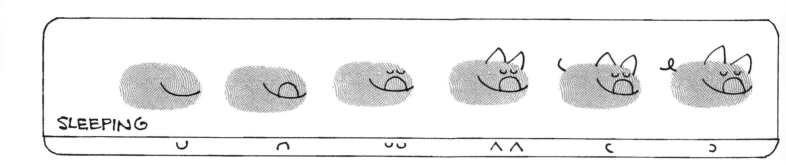

SLEEPING

∪   ∩   ∪∪   ∧ ∧   ℂ   Ɔ

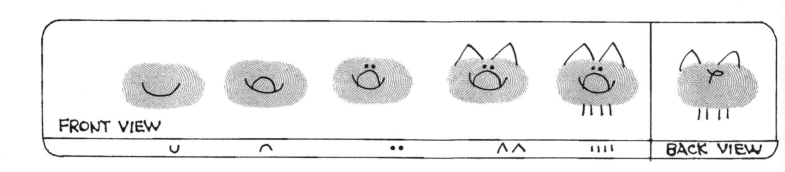

FRONT VIEW

∪   ∩   ••   ∧ ∧   ‖‖   BACK VIEW

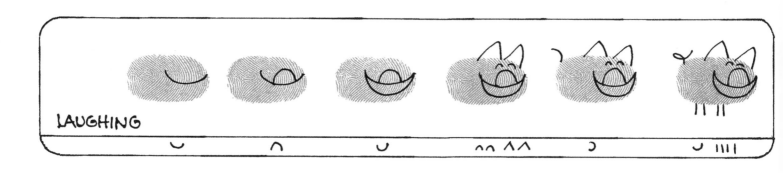

LAUGHING

∪   ∩   ∪   ∩∩ ∧∧   Ɔ   ∪ ‖‖

WORRIED   ANGRY   SITTING DOWN   SINGING   PIGLET   JUMPING OVER

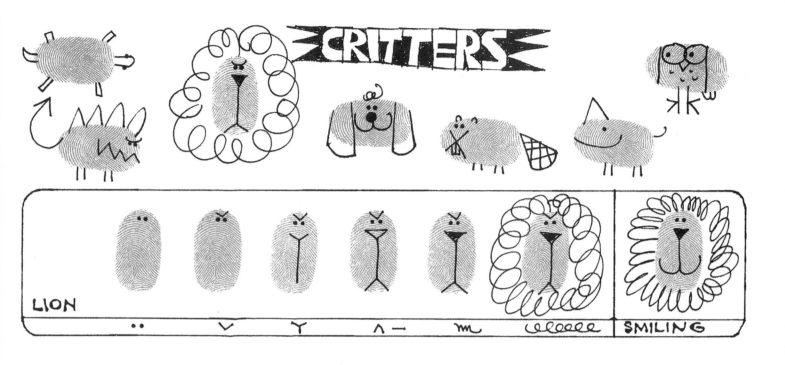

CRITTERS

LION							SMILING
••	∨	Y	∧ —	ɯ	ℓℓℓℓℓℓ		SMILING

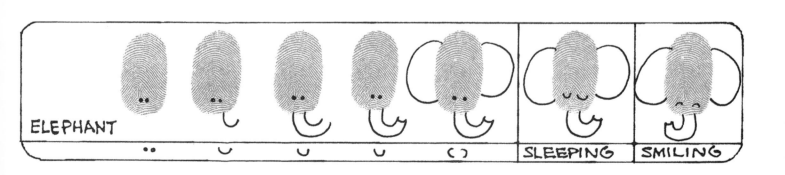

CAT							WINKING
••	∨	∪∪	— ∧∧	∪ ∪∪ ∪∪	≡ ≡		WINKING

ELEPHANT					SLEEPING	SMILING
••	∪	∪	∪	( )	SLEEPING	SMILING

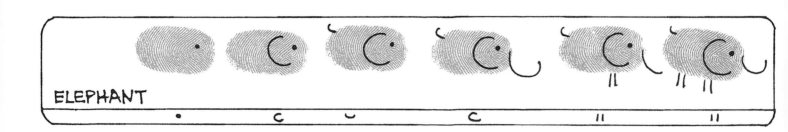

ELEPHANT

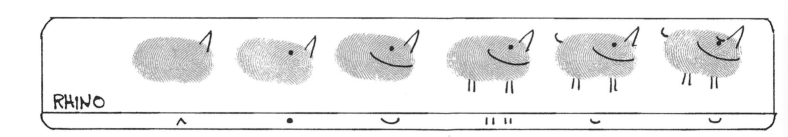

RHINO

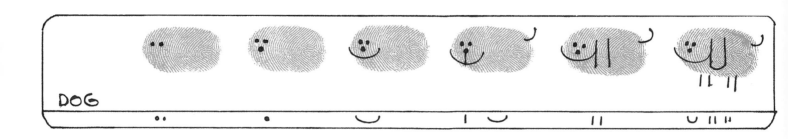

DOG

MONSTER

BEAVER

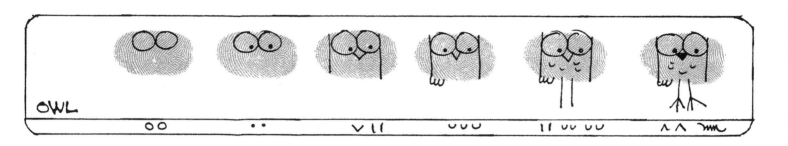

OWL

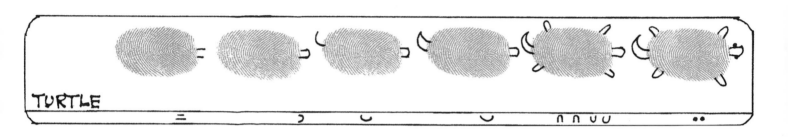

TURTLE

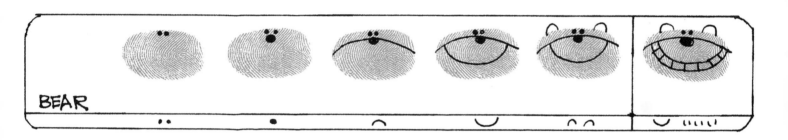

BEAR

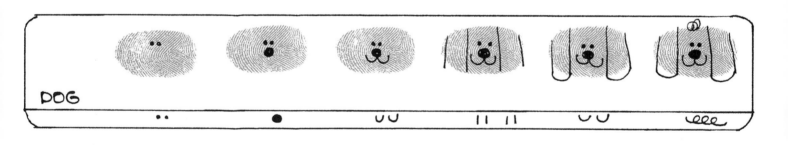

DOG

HAMSTER

HAMSTER
TOP VIEW

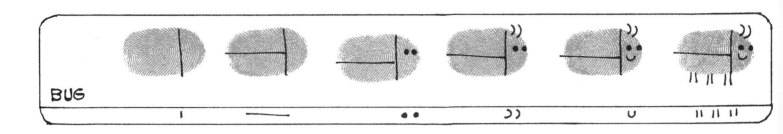

BUG

BEE

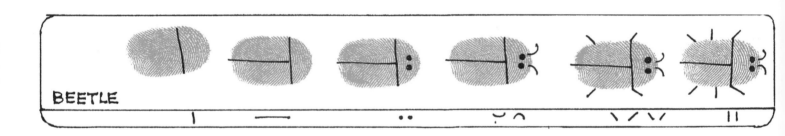

BEETLE

CATERPILLAR

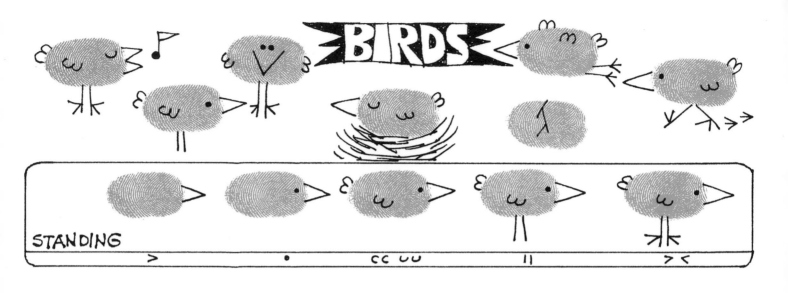

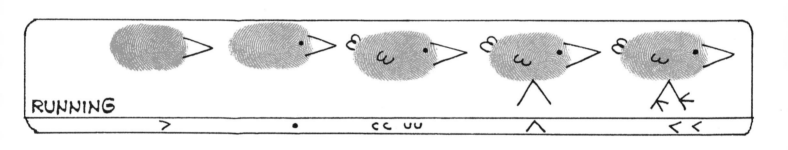

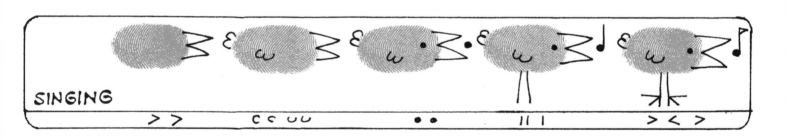

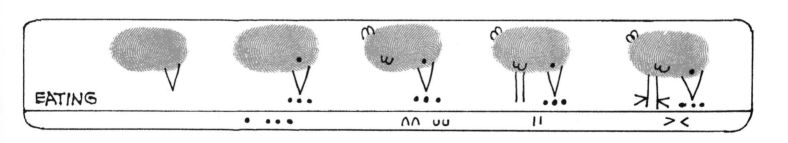

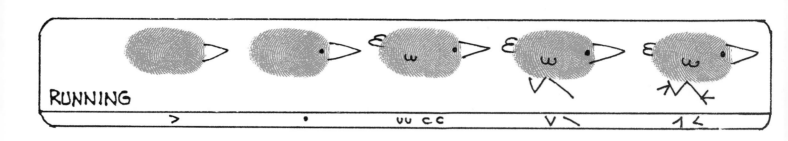

RUNNING

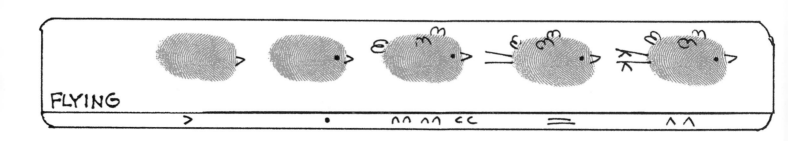

FLYING

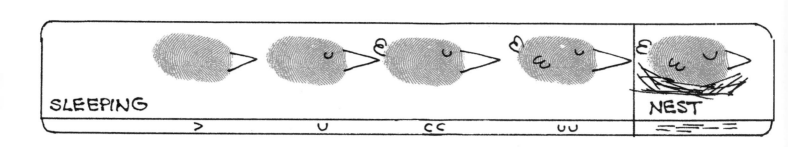

SLEEPING   NEST

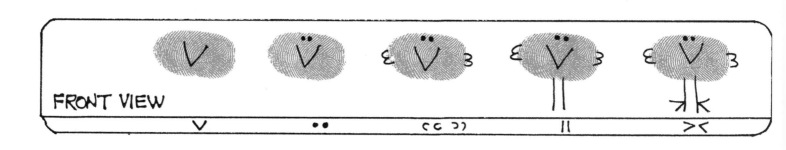

FRONT VIEW

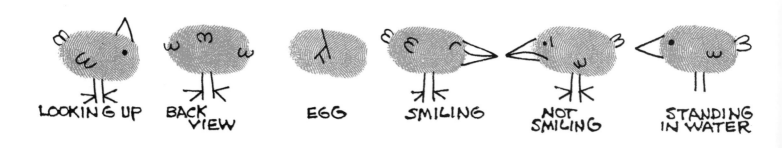

LOOKING UP   BACK VIEW   EGG   SMILING   NOT SMILING   STANDING IN WATER

HOLIDAYS

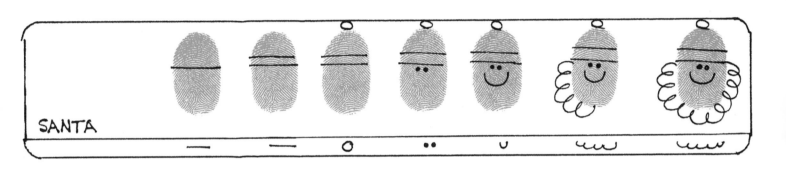

SANTA

FIRECRACKER

BIRTHDAY CAKE

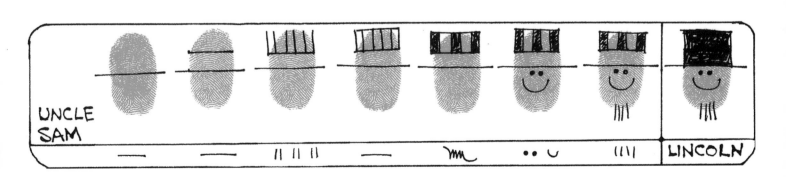

UNCLE SAM

LINCOLN

HALLOWEEN

HALLOWEEN

GEORGE
WASHINGTHUMB

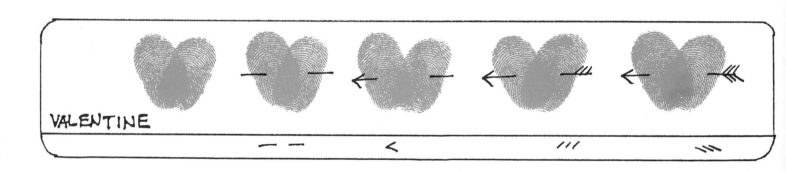

VALENTINE

26

PILGRIM

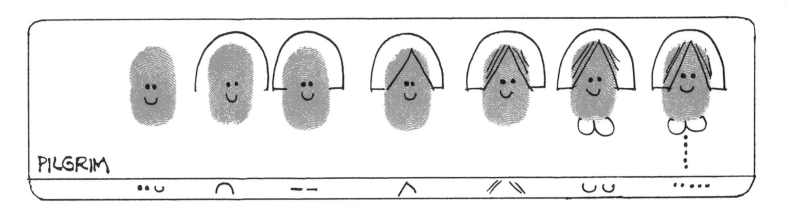

PILGRIM

EASTER
BUNNY

FLOWERS

MORE THUMBS

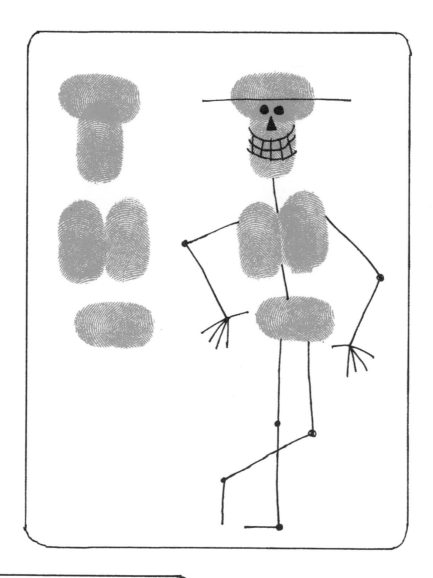

THIS AND THAT

THE GARDEN

FLOWER

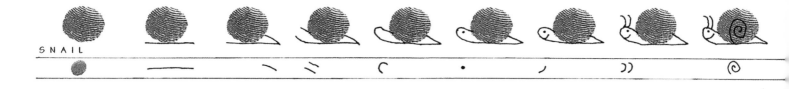

SNAIL

FROG

SMALL FLOWER

CROCUS

TULIP

BROWN ANT

CATERPILLAR

CENTIPEDE

BUMBLEBEE

THE POND

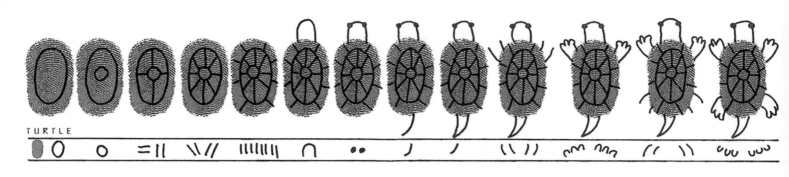

TURTLE

DUCK

POLLYWOG

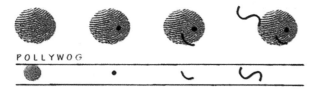

BUTTERFLY

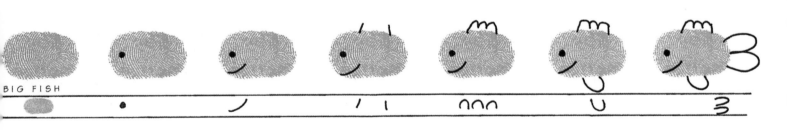

SWIMMING FROG

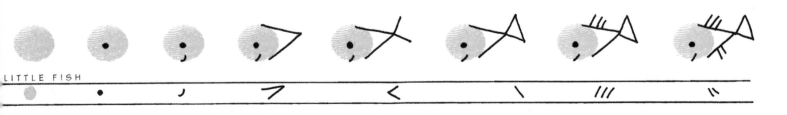

BIG FISH

LITTLE FISH

FINGERLINGS

I ALSO CALL THESE MY
TEENY TINIES. I USE A
DIFFERENT FINGERTIP FOR
EACH COLOR.

SPRING

SUMMER

RABBIT

MOUSE

OWL   FROG   DOG

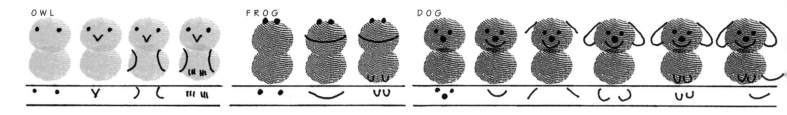

BEAVER

FALL　　FALL　　WINTER

SITTING CAT

BIRD

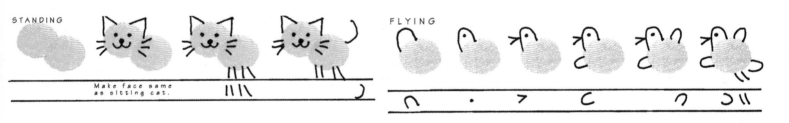

STANDING

Make face same
as sitting cat.

FLYING

RUNNING

Make face same
as sitting cat.

PECKING

ANIMALS

ELEPHANT

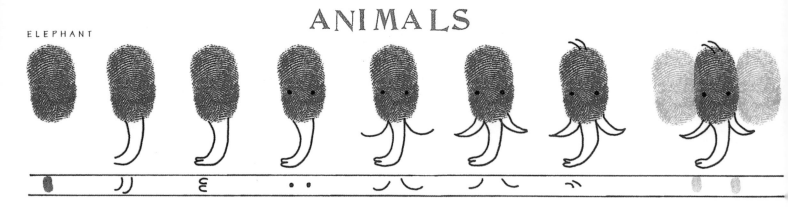

BABY ELEPHANT

LION

40

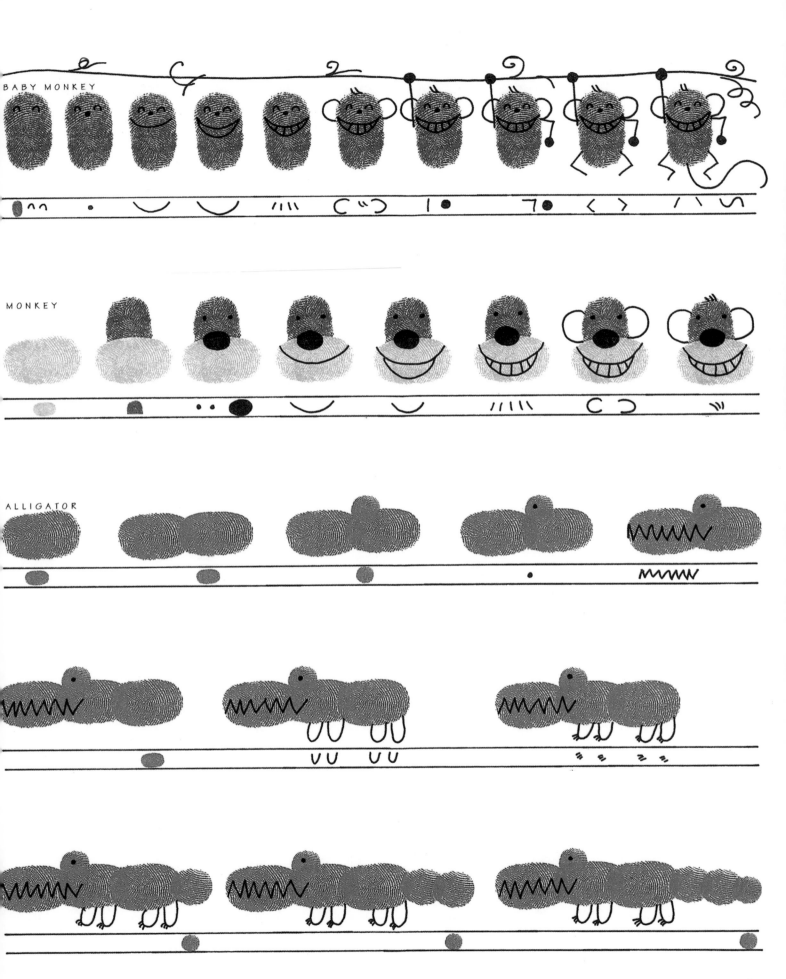

BABY MONKEY

MONKEY

ALLIGATOR

MORE ANIMALS

RACCOON

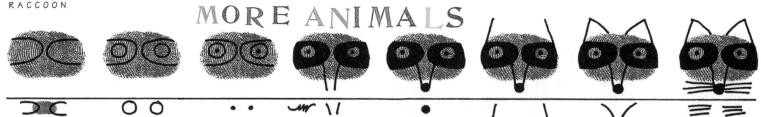

PIG

BEAVER

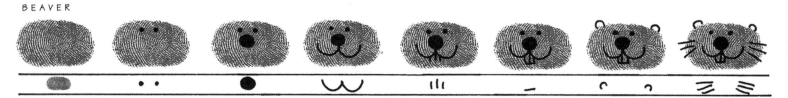

DOG

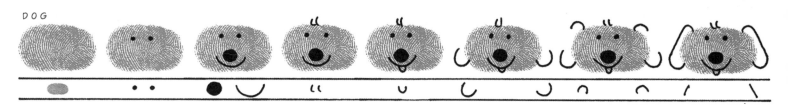

CAT

SMALL BULLDOG

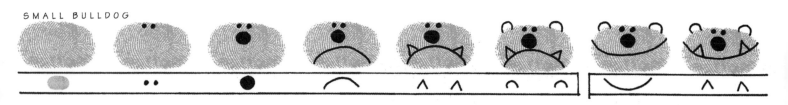

MOUSE

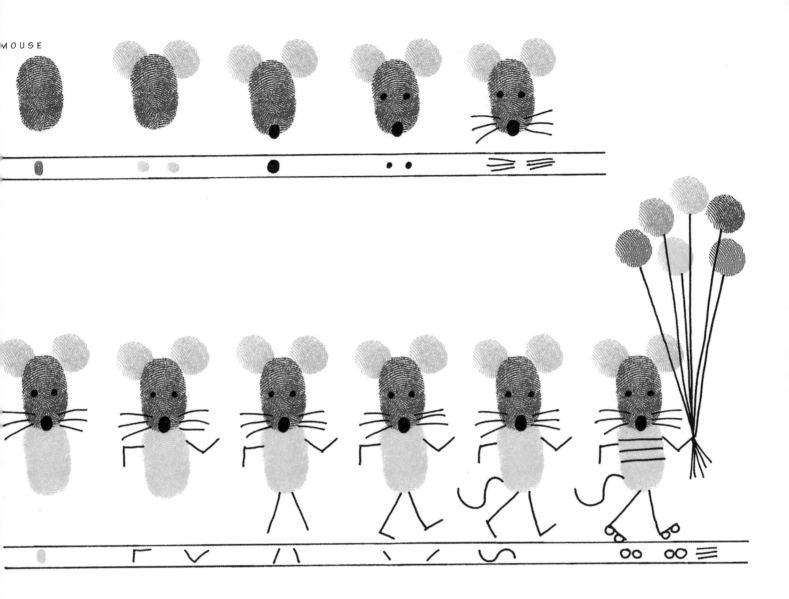

BIG BULLDOG

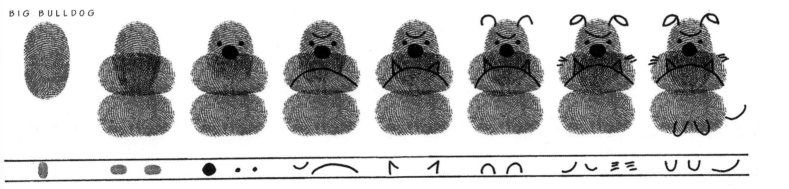

43

BIRDS

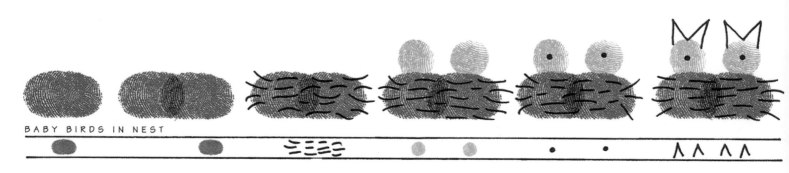

BABY BIRDS IN NEST

BIRD EATING WORM

BIRD FRONT VIEW

BIRD BACK VIEW

BIRD FLYING

BIRD SINGING

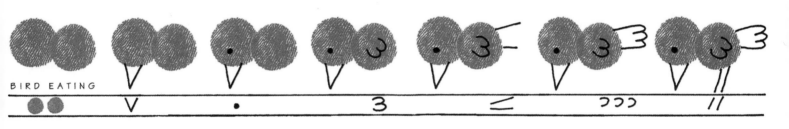

BIRD EATING

BIRD WALKING

BEAN BUDDIES

I THINK FINGERPRINTS LOOK LIKE LITTLE BEANS. I LIKE TO USE THESE LITTLE "FINGER BEANS" TO MAKE ALL DIFFERENT KINDS OF LITTLE BEAN BUDDIES.

BASIC

PEA BEAN BUDDY   BAKED BEAN BUDDY   LIMA BEAN BUDDY   JELLY BEAN BUDDY

SPEAKING

•• ◡ — ‖ / -- — ∫ ◡ HI!

POINTING

•• ◡ — ‖ / (LOOK ☆

YAWNING

⌢⌢ ◯ ‖ \ / HO HUM

CELEBRATING

⌢⌢ ◡ — / \ \ / \/ \ HOORA

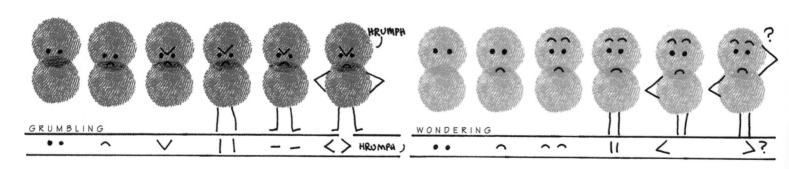

GRUMBLING

•• ⌃ ∨ ‖ — — ⟨ ⟩ HRUMPH

WONDERING

•• ⌢ ⌢⌢ ‖ ⟨ ⟩ ?

46

WALKING

JOGGING

RUNNING

WINNING

BALLET

HULA

CLOG
DANCING

TAP DANCING

LITTLE CLOWN

NAPOLEON

SAILOR

QUEEN   KING   PRINCE

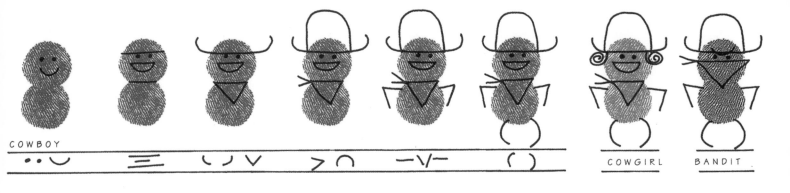

COWBOY

•• ⌣   ☰   ∪∪∨   >∩   —∨—   ( )   COWGIRL   BANDIT

PIRATE

— ☰   •∪∩   >o⌣⌣ |⊔   ´| /\   \ /•—

SUPERPERSON

☰—   —••   /\∪   ∪   \ /   ◁ ◁   •• SP   // ∧

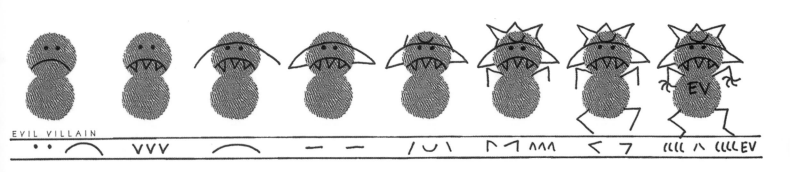

EVIL VILLAIN

•• ⌒   VVV   ⌒   — —   /∪\   ⌐⌐ ΛΛΛ   < 7   ⟨⟨⟨ ∧ ⟨⟨⟨⟨EV

FEELINGS

HAPPY

VERY HAPPY

VERY VERY HAPPY

SNOOTY
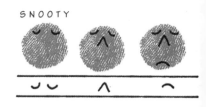

SAD
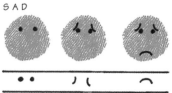

VERY SAD

VERY VERY SAD
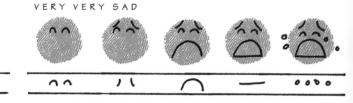

UPSET

ANGRY

VERY ANGRY

VERY VERY ANGRY

SLY (MISCHIEVOUS)

SHY (EMBARRASSED)
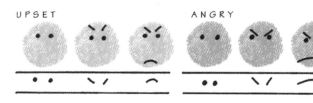

SUSPICIOUS

HURTING

OUCH
OUCH

MUSIC

HUMMING
MMM

WHISTLING

SINGING
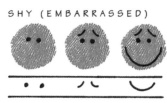

SINGERS
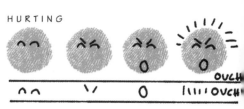

MMM

50

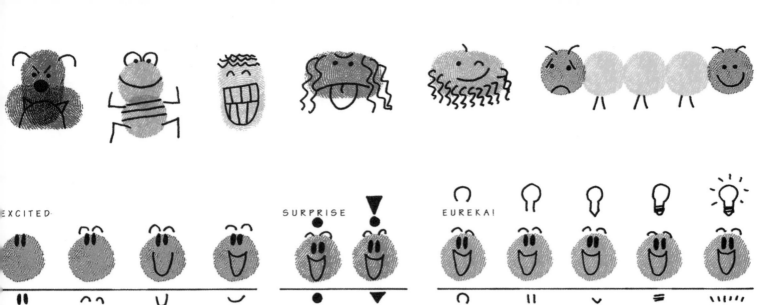

EXCITED

SURPRISE

EUREKA!

|| ∩∩ ∪ ⌣

• ▼

∩ || ⌄ = \\\\\\

PUZZLED

IN LOVE

BOP!

•• ⌢⌣ ⌢ ?

•• ⌣⌣ ∪ ♡♡♡

⌢ ×× ○ ⋯ ☆☆ BOP!

SLEEPY

ASLEEP

SNORING

SICK

•• ⌣⌣ ⌢

⌣⌣ ∪

⌣⌣ ● ZZZ

•• ⌣⌣ ⌣⌣⌣ ⋰⋱

COLD

HOT

HELP!

•• ⌣⌣ ⌢ ⌇⌇ ⌇⌇

•• ⌣⌣ ⌢ ◗◗ ⌇⌇

⌣⌣ ⌣⌣ ⌢ ⌣ HELP!

HUNGRY

YUK!

PHOOEY!

•• ⌣⌣ ∪ ⌣ YUM YUM

•• ∪ ⌢ ∪ ,

•• ⌣ ⌢ ∪ |

51

SPRING FUN

SKIPPING ROPE

BICYCLING

SKATEBOARDING

ROLLER-SKATING

APRIL SHOWERS

FISHING

HIKING

KITES

SUMMER FUN

CHASING BUTTERFLIES

SWIMMING

SURFING

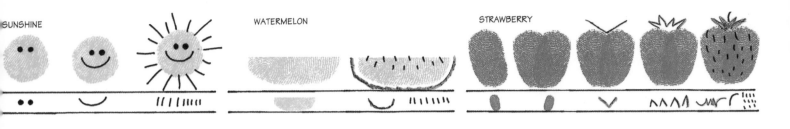

SUNSHINE

WATERMELON

STRAWBERRY

LAWN MOWING

SUNBATHING

BASEBALL

FALL FUN

 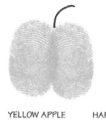  

APPLE

PEAR

YELLOW APPLE   HAPPY GREEN APPLE   GRAPES

FARMING

LACROSSE

SOCCER

56

FOOTBALL

SPORTS FAN

CHEERLEADER

BASKETBALL

57

WINTER FUN

PENGUIN FRONT VIEW

PENGUIN SIDE VIEW

SNOWPERSON

SKIING

SKATING

HOCKEY

HOLIDAYS

EASTER BUNNY

EASTER EGG

CHOCOLATE EGG

CHICK

VALENTINE

SHAMROCK

LEPRECHAUN

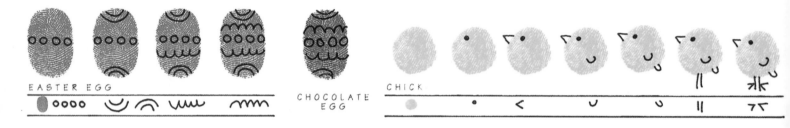

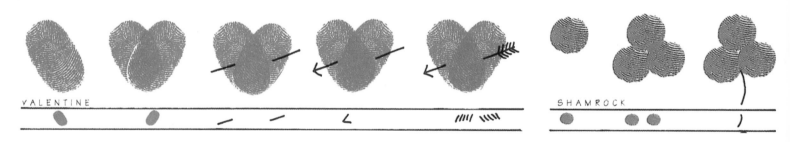

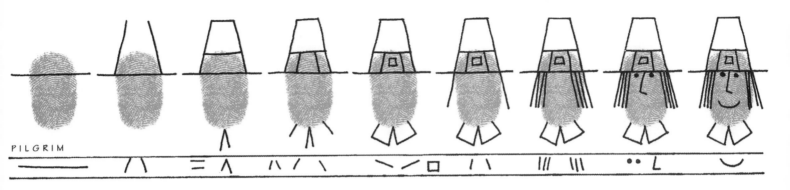

PILGRIM

TURKEY

PILGRIM

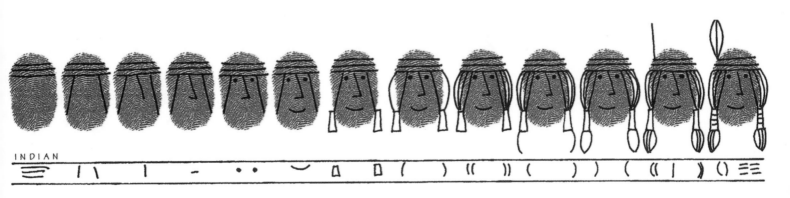

INDIAN

HALLOWEEN

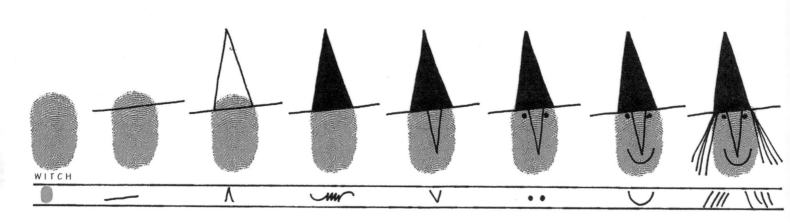

WITCH

FLYING WITCH

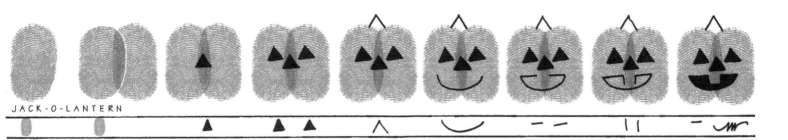

JACK-O-LANTERN

BAT

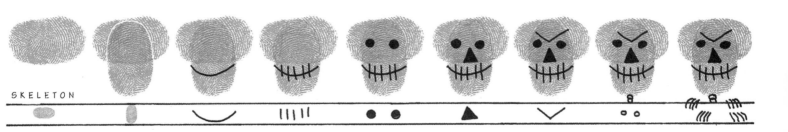

SKELETON

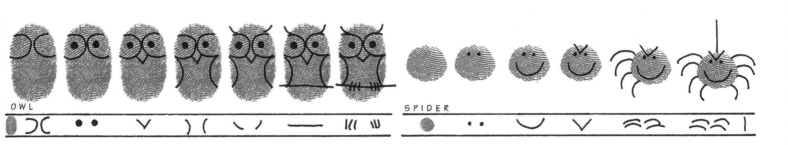

OWL   SPIDER

CAT

63

*DASHER * DANCER * PRANCER * VIXEN *

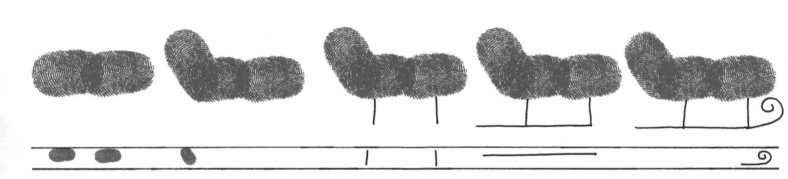

JINGLE   JINGLE   JINGLE

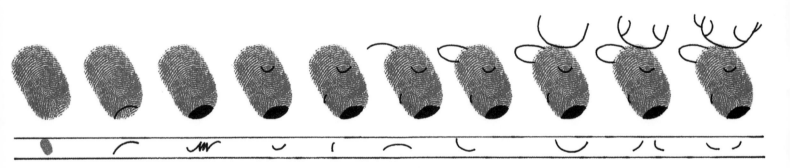

LAND SEA AND AIR

CAR

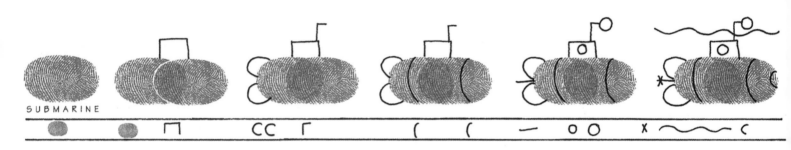

SUBMARINE

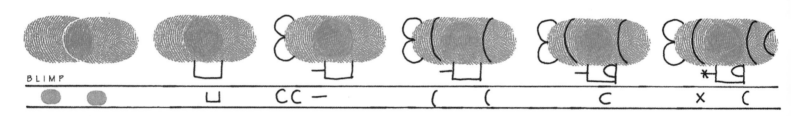

BLIMP

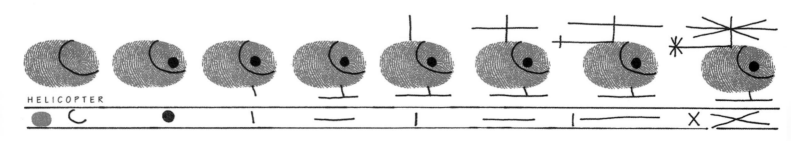

HELICOPTER

TRAIN

ENGINE

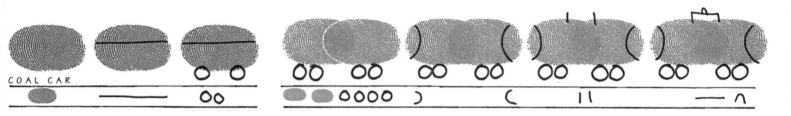

COAL CAR

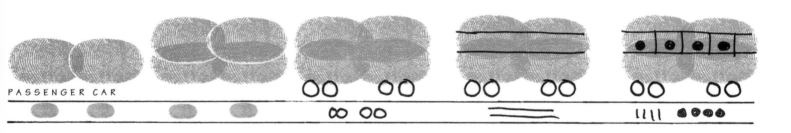

PASSENGER CAR

FREIGHT CAR

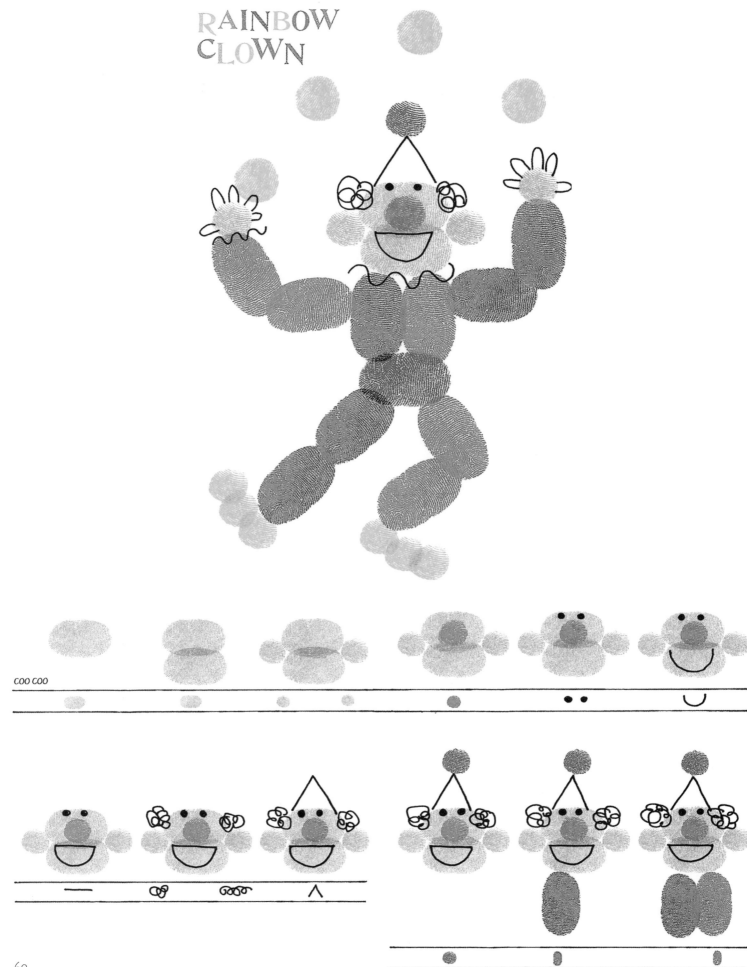

RAINBOW CLOWN

COO COO

68

FESTER

LULU

RAINBOW DRAGON

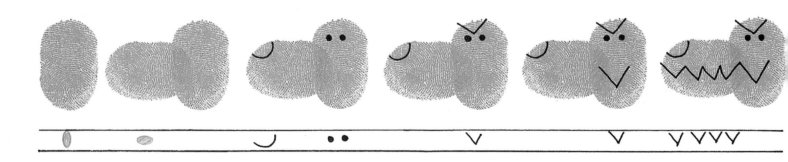

LION

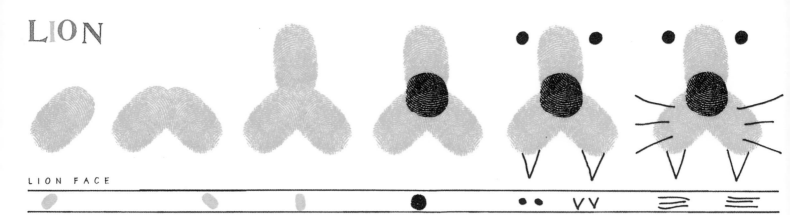

LION FACE

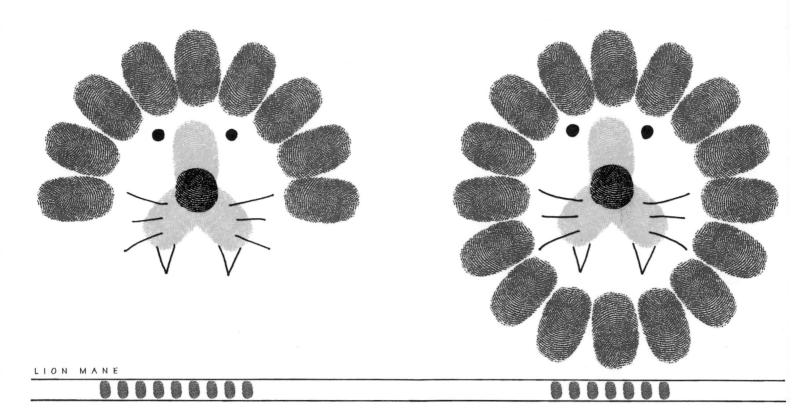

LION MANE

RAINBOW
LIONS

SKETCH BOOK

HERE ARE SOME FINGERPRINT
THINGS I COULD NOT FIT INTO THIS
BOOK. CAN YOU FIGURE OUT HOW
I MADE THEM?

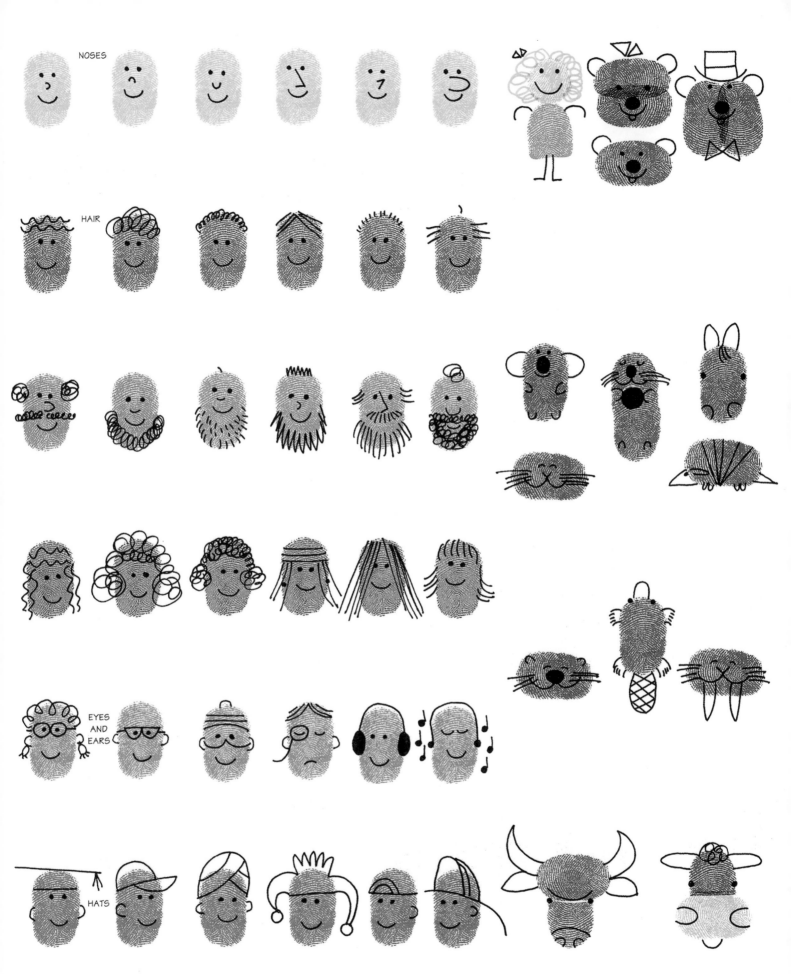

NOSES

HAIR

EYES AND EARS

HATS

75

ADVANCED FINGER-PRINTING

FOR THE ADVENTUROUS—
JUST A FEW OTHER WAYS TO COMBINE PRINTS,
COLORS, SIMPLE LINES, AND SOME
IMAGINATION TO MAKE PICTURES.
THERE ARE LOTS LEFT FOR YOU TO DISCOVER.
HAPPY DISCOVERING!

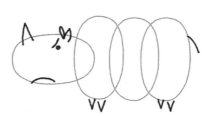

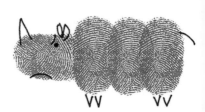

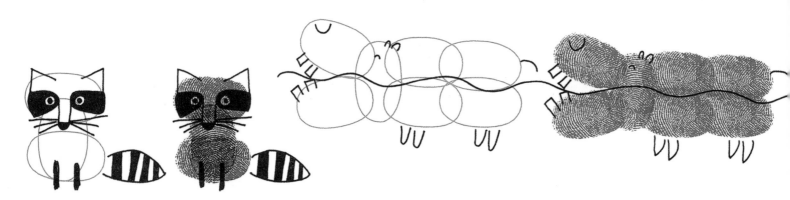

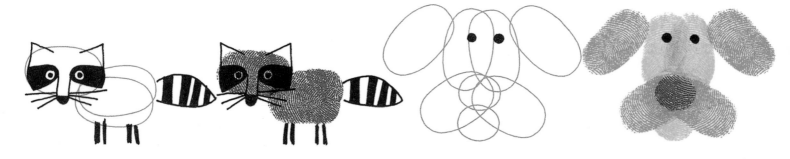

Something very special.

Just as no two fingerprints look just alike, no two fingerprint pictures will ever look just alike. Prints will be lighter or darker, lines will be thicker or thinner, colors will be different.

That means that no other fingerprint pictures will look just like the ones in this book, or just like yours. That's what will make your pictures "something very special."

More Ed Emberley Drawing Book Fun!

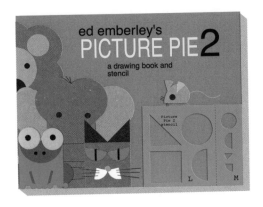

ED EMBERLEY'S DRAWING BOOK
OF ANIMALS

ED EMBERLEY'S DRAWING BOOK
OF FACES

ED EMBERLEY'S PICTURE PIE,
A CUT AND PASTE DRAWING BOOK

ED EMBERLEY'S PICTURE PIE TWO,
A DRAWING BOOK AND STENCIL

THE WING ON A FLEA:
A BOOK ABOUT SHAPES

ED EMBERLEY'S DRAWING BOOK,
MAKE A WORLD

ED EMBERLEY'S
BIG GREEN DRAWING BOOK
ED EMBERLEY'S
BIG ORANGE DRAWING BOOK
ED EMBERLEY'S
BIG PURPLE DRAWING BOOK
ED EMBERLEY'S BIG
RED DRAWING BOOK

DINOSAURS, A DRAWING BOOK
BY MICHAEL EMBERLEY

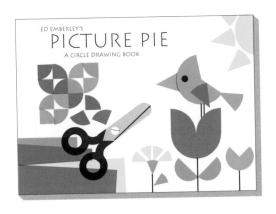

Little Brown and Company
Time Warner Book Group
1271 Avenue of the Americas, New York, NY 10020
Visit our Web site at www.lb-kids.com

First Edition

From the previously published books by Ed Emberley
GREAT THUMBPRINT DRAWING BOOK (copyright © 1977)
and
THE FINGERPRINT DRAWING BOOK (copyright © 2000)

ISBN 0-316-17448-3

10 9 8 7 6

SC

Manufactured in China